Wind of the Journey

Other English translation books by Irina Ratushinskaya

Poetry Collections

No, I'm Not Afraid
Beyond the Limit
Pencil Letter
Dance with a Shadow

Prose

Grey is the Color of Hope
A Tale of Three Heads
In the Beginning
The Odessans
Fictions and Lies

Wind of the Journey

Poems by
Irina Ratushinskaya

Translated by
Lydia Razran Stone

Cornerstone Press Chicago
Chicago, Illinois

Wind of the Journey

First edition

Published by Cornerstone Press Chicago
939 W. Wilson Ave.
Chicago, IL 60640
cspress@jpusa.org
www.cornerstonepress.com

Cover photo by Terry Wheeler

Cover design and book design by Scott Stahnke

Thank you to Paul Hanover, Maynard Kabak, and Debbie Shulman, and Karl Natschke at Digital Publishing Group for color separations and helping us to find a qualified translator.

Printed in the United States of America
ISBN 0-940895-44-7

05 04 03 02 01 00 5 4 3 2 1

Library of Congress Cataloging-in-Publication Data

Ratushinskaia, Irina.
    [Poems. English & Russian. Selections]
    Wind of the journey : poems / by Irina Ratushinskaya.
        p. cm.
    Parallel text in English and Russian.
    Translated by Lydia Razran Stone.
    ISBN 0-940895-44-7
    1. Ratushinskaĕi, Irina--Translations into English. I. Stone, Lydia Razran. II. Title.
    PG3485.5.A875 A27 2000
    891.71'4.4—dc21   00-029489

Contents

Editors' Note

Irina Ratushinskaya will forever be known as the poet who was arrested for her poetry, sentenced to a Soviet prison camp, and who continued in the face of persecution to write new poems. She wrote them on bars of soap, memorized them, and then washed away the "evidence." Irina is a recognized poet in both the international community and the United States.

Cornerstone Press Chicago is proud to bring out a new collection of Irina's poems. We first learned of Irina when she was jailed for publishing her poetry in uncensored publications. Irina came to write poetry only after obtaining her degree in physics in 1976. She was influenced at the time by the poets of the Russian Silver Age—Mandelstam, Akhmatova, Pasternak, and Tsvetayeva. In 1979 she married Igor Geraschenko and together they became involved with the human rights movement in Russia which led the KGB to examine her poetry. A number of poems in this collection represent her time in prison from 1982 until 1986 when the International Pen Congress agitated for her release.

When freed on October 9, 1986, she was physically broken. After her release Irina taught as a visiting professor at Northwestern University in the United States (1987–1989) before moving to England to pursue writing full-time. A gap between 1991 and 1995 in her poems can be attributed to the birth of her twin sons, Oleg and Sergei, born in 1992. Some poems in this collection were written mainly for her children. In late 1998 President Yeltsin restored Irina's citizenship, and she and her family were permitted to return to Russia. Today they live in Moscow.

Since 1992 the poetry world has not heard from Irina. This collection, *Wind of the Journey,* will let her many readers see how her writing has matured. Many of Irina's newer poems tell the story of her journey out of imprisonment into a changing world of estrangement and exile. From a faith forged through suffering Irina shows that one lives by dying, one grows stronger by suffering.

As editors, we wanted to remain faithful to Irina's words and images. To do this we set before us three goals listed according to their importance:

We wanted to capture as completely as possible (both emotively and cognitively) the content (metaphor, punctuation, word usage etc.) of Irina's poetry.

In presenting Irina's poems, we wanted to be aware of American sensibilities. We decided it was more important to get Irina's thought across than to introduce readers to Russian style poetry. Thus, at times we "corrected" passages that might appear confusing or trite in English. There are several poems where we chose to go with a free verse translation rather than the formal only because the rendering seemed more on the mark.

And, finally, we wanted to retain where possible the rhyme and meter of Irina's poems. The form that Irina chose had a lot to do with the meaning she intended to portray. Thus, many of the poems in this collection have remained in the tradition of rhymed poetry.

We knew we wouldn't be able to satisfy all criteria, but to meet these goals we employed some basic guidelines:

We compared the literal translation of each poem closely with the proposed English poem to make sure the metaphors and other figures of speech made it into the translation. Sometimes in working to get the rhythm and rhyme correct we were tempted to explain a metaphor. We tried hard not to do that, leaving Irina's images to be interpreted by her readers.

For those readers who are interested in the art of poetry, we believe this edition of Irina's poetry is unique. Russian poetry follows poetic conventions more closely than American poetry. The anapest foot tends to dominate. The lines may contain any number of feet and the rhythm is quite regular. Those who have kept up with Irina's poetry will be interested in comparing the newer poems with those written before and during her imprisonment. One might wonder how freedom has impacted or improved her verse.

Some of the poems are titled, some are not. The reason for this inconsistency is that Irina only gave three or four poems titles and left the rest untitled. We asked if we could title two of the poems, "Dog Who Does Not Exist" and "Recipe for a Planet". Irina assured us that Russian poetry is often untitled, perhaps leaving that up to the reader. Nonetheless, we needed a way to identify the untitled poems and decided to number the poems in this collection.

Many of Irina's poems have the earmarks of a well-seasoned traveller: an eagerness for adventure, melancholy good-byes, and insight into the ends of journeys. Irina uses images as icons, weaving in themes such as life in prison, the coming of spring, and her Orthodox faith. Her pictures transcend language, impressing upon the reader emotions and yearnings universal to all. In *Lectures on Russian Literature* Vladimir Nabokov explained it this way, ". . . Literature is not a pattern of ideas but a pattern of images. Ideas do not matter much in comparison to a book's imagery and magic. . . . Let us keep an eye on the imagery and leave the ideas to pile up as they please. The word, the expression, the image is the true function of literature. Not ideas."

Another method Irina makes frequent use of is understatement, which can be easily misunderstood if not read correctly. Irina states, "There is a common problem with understatements—when explained boldly they sound flat and primitive. In Russian fairy tales there is a favorite character, Ivan Durak. Take away the reputation of an idiot from these tales, stop Ivan from playing an immature, trusting, easy-to-fool, impractical big child—and you will have a plain story of success. Some people miss the understatement and think that an idiot is the true Russian hero. As one of my friends, a politician, said, 'Our main state secret is that we are not idiots. Let us keep it and let people think what they want.' "

Irina Ratushinskaya, in keeping with the true meaning of parables, has taken that which seems simple and mundane, and plunged it into a sea of metaphors and images, striking a cord within us all.

Curt Mortimer
Jane Hertenstein
Cornerstone Press Chicago

Nabokov, Vladimir. *Lectures in Russian Literature*. Edited by Fredson Bowers. New York: Harcourt Brace Jovanovich, 1982.

Translator's Note

It has been not only an honor, but a real pleasure, to collaborate with Irina Ratushinskaya on the translations of the poems in this volume and to work with Jane Hertenstein and Curt Mortimer to polish the translations. I would describe the process of translating poetry as "a series of compromises punctuated by miracles." What the compromises are about is probably pretty obvious. As in all translation, one has to render the author's meaning, both his or her communicative and expressive intentions, and at least to some extent, the words selected to communicate those intentions and do it in relatively smooth, grammatical language, taking account of any relevant differences between the two cultures. This may not be an easy task even for straightforward communications, and it is a great deal more difficult when there is a complex relationship between an author's meaning and the words and images selected to convey it, as there is in poetry. If one is working with rhymed, metric poetry, like the majority of poems in this collection, one has to think in addition about how to reproduce the rhyme scheme and rhythm, often (and this is certainly true of Russian and English) working with languages that are very dissimilar in inherent sound and stress pattern. Given all these constraints, it is not surprising that in translating poetry one is constantly having to compromise and settle for a less than perfect rendition of meaning, smooth English phrase, reproduction of meter or even (perish the thought), less than exact rhymes. Indeed, one would think that it would be absolutely impossible to produce a perfect translation, and only slightly less impossible, to produce one that was good enough. This is where the other part of definition comes in. If you truly love poetry and the particular poems you are trying to translate and if you work on them hard enough and long enough, every once in a while you are granted a near-miracle, a line or even a stanza, or once in a great while, most of a whole poem, that is, if not perfect, at least so close to good enough as to defy the odds against producing such a thing. After having one or two of these experiences, you become addicted.

The majority of the original poems in this collection are formal as well as semantic objects; in other words, they are marked by certain specific patterns of rhyme and rhythm, although frequently these patterns do not correspond to standard patterns in English poetry. To the best of my ability, I have tried to render these formal features. In the majority of instances, miraculously and with help from the author and my editors, I have been, I think, relatively successful in this. In certain instances, we felt that we could not reproduce form without impairing meaning, and these poems were translated into blank verse. Occasionally, the final form of the translated poem owes as much to the editors, Jane Hertenstein and Curt Mortimer, as to me. I want to thank them for their help in particular with poem Thirty-one. Of course, all three of us, Curt, Jane, and I are extremely grateful to Irina Ratushinskaya, not only for writing these beautiful words, but for participating so enthusiastically and actively in the translation process: explaining cultural allusions and latent meaning in great detail, and determining which aspects of form or meaning could be stretched a bit for the benefit of rendering others.

Lydia Razran Stone

Wind of
the
Journey

Киев

Этот вечер для долгой прогулки.
Серый час, как домашняя кошка,
Теплой тенью скользит у колена,
А подъезды печальны и гулки.
Ты надень свою старую куртку.
Мы набьем леденцами карманы
И пойдем, куда хочется сердцу,
Безо всякого дельного плана.
По заросшим ромашкой кварталам,
Где трамвай уже больше не ходит,
Где открытые низкие окна,
Но старушек в них прежних не стало.
Так мы выйдем к знакомому дому
И увидим на спущенной шторе
Тень хозяина, и улыбнемся:
Кто сегодня в гостях, с кем он спорит?
Мы замедлим шаги: не зайти ли?
Но заманят нас сумерки дальше,
Уведут, как детишек цыгане,
Как уже много раз уводили.
И тогда, заблудившись, как дети,
В незнакомом обоим предместье -
Вдруг очнемся: мы живы и вместе!
И вернемся домой на рассвете.

1984

one

Kiev

Just the night for a walk; let's get going
While the dusk, gray-ghost cat, settles in,
Purrs and winds, shadowlike, round your shin;
And our hallway's forlorn and echoing.
Go and get on your shabby old vest.
Take along all the candy you can.
We will roam at our spirits' behest;
Walk without any purpose or plan.
Where the trolleys have long ceased to run,
We will stroll past some overgrown square.
Though the low ground floor windows are there,
The old wives watching from them are gone.
Later on, shadows cast on the curtain
In the house of our friend may distract us.
"There's good talk there tonight—that's certain."
But for now dropping in doesn't attract us.
Only walking tonight seems appealing
As the twilight keeps beckoning, luring us.
We have done this before, there's no curing us.
We're like children the gypsies are stealing.
Then, like children, we find we are stranded
In some suburb we've not seen before, ever.
The spell lifts: we're alive and together.
We'll get home by the time night has ended.

Возьмемте Моцарта с собой
Во многомильную дорогу,
Простого счастия залогом
Возьмемте Моцарта с собой!

Не надо вещи паковать:
Они истлеют под дождями,
И повстречавшиеся с ними
Друзья не будут узнавать.

Нам будет ветер как огонь,
Колодец будет как награда,
И скудных сумерек прохлада -
Как доброй мачехи ладонь.

Возьмемте Моцарта с собой:
Все остальное будет лишним.
Ведь мы за скрипкой не услышим,
Когда нам протрубят отбой.

1988

two

And, Mozart let us take along.
One simple joy we'll thus ensure
On this long road we must endure.
Remember, bring Mozart along.

Don't pack fine clothes. What use are they?
They'll only rot in heat and rain.
And if we meet our friends again
They will not know us anyway.

The wind that blows across the sand
Will be our only fire now.
The pallid dusk will cool our brow—
A kind stepmother's soothing hand.

So, Mozart let us take along.
There's nothing else that we will need.
We will not hear them play retreat,
While Mozart fills our head with song.

Ах, как наша планета мучительно невелика:
Все ребячьи качели похожи одни на другие,
И все так же гуляют по душам четыре стихии,
И все так же внимательно смотрят на нас облака.

Мы въезжаем в весну, и сужаются рельсы на юг,
Но на север направлены птичьи тревожные стаи.
Мы апреля не ждем,
Но сердцами в него прорастаем -
Так счастливо и трудно, как будто во славу Твою.

1987

three

Oh, how small is our planet,
How miserably small and confined:
All the swings used by children
Have just the same shape everywhere
While the selfsame four elements
Buffet our souls when they rage.
In each place from the clouds
We're attentively watched just the same.

It is spring when we leave
And our train tracks converge to the south,
Although birds' restless flocks
Are all headed due north overhead.
In our hearts we're not waiting
For April but growing toward it.
Oh, 'tis joyful and hard
Like all journeys we make for Your glory.

Ну что ж, весна!
Улыбка обезьянки.
Лукавые очистки апельсинов,
Портовый воздух между влажных стен.
Нам ворожат
Печальные цыганки,
И мы во сне вдыхаем, обессилев,
Предчувствие дождей и перемен.
Ну что ж, пора. . .

1979

four

Spring comes sudden to this clime:
The sailors' pet monkeys revive;
Port streets are littered with bright orange rind
Whose fragrance blends with pungent sea air.
Sad-eyed gypsies arrive
Observe our palms and say all will be fine.
Our sleep is restless with hope and despair
Foreshadows of rain and of change fill the mind.
Is it not time. . . ?

Что календарь? Формальность бытия!
Любой февраль уже сиренью дует.
И прежнюю печаль на молодую
Под буйную крамолу воронья
Сменяет. Но приросшая - болит!
Скребут асфальту шкуру.
Соль земли
Разметена по влажным тротуарам.
Цветные сны слоятся тонким паром,
А мы отвыкли радости делить.
Как женщина неловкая - пакеты,
Мы их роняем - всей охапкой - в снег.
Но все равно хватает всем, на всех!
О перемен прозрачная примета!
О времени веселое весло!
Промокших варежек наивное тепло
Впечатается в корочку сугроба,
Зашмыгают иззябшие микробы,
Весенние созвездья из берлог
Подымут легкий запах нафталина,
И Бог, слепив дитя из мокрой глины,
Остатками запрудит ручеек.

1983

five

The calendar? A mere convention
When February's breath can seem like May's.
With brand new griefs the old ones we replace
To raucous sounds of crows' contention.
But scabs adhere and hurt—no one escapes
Renewal's pain. The sidewalks too get scraped
And sprinkled with the earth's salt here and there.
Bright dreams, like steam, rise up in warming air.
We can't share joys—we've lost the knack.
We fumble them and in the snow they fall,
As if freed from some too-full paper sack.
And yet there is enough, enough for all.
Oh airy sign of change before our eyes!
Oh merry oar to use when rivers flow!
Oh mark of mittened palm in melting snow!
Dormant microbes wake, warm up with exercise.
While constellations leave their lairs to forage
They smell of mothballed fur that's been in storage.
And having brought new babes to life today
God dams up ponds to use leftover clay.

Сойдем с ума печальною весной,
Когда снега вздыхают об апреле,
Когда уже грозит подрыв основ
Сугробам, и камины догорели,
Когда стоит над нами Орион,
Но наплывают странные созвездья,
Когда из мира не приходят вести,
Но он такой душою одарен,
Что прорывается в молчание утрат -
С ума сойти! Какого ветра милость?
Вот так проснешься как-нибудь с утра -
И все исполнится,
Как только что приснилось.

1984

six

This melancholy spring, let's lose our minds
As snows dissolve in tears for April yearning.
The hardest drifts will soon be undermined;
The fires on our hearths will finish burning.
Orion stands above and yet we sense
The advent of some strange new constellation,
Though from the world there comes no information.
It has a soul that breaches every fence
And penetrates our silence with its light.
What mad wind's blown such miracles this way?
If this keeps on, we'll wake to find, one day,
All wishes coming true, as in our dream last night.

А в этом году подуло весной
Четвертого февраля.
И на вспененной лошади вестовой
В нелепом мундире старинных войн
Промчал по мерзлым полям.
Прокатили мускулы облаков
По всем горизонтам гром.
И запели трубы былых полков
Смертью и серебром.
И по грудь в весне провели коней,
И намокли весной плащи,
А что там могло так странно звенеть -
Мне было не различить.
Но рвануло сердце на этот звон,
И усталость крылом смело.
И это был никакой не сон:
Было уже светло.

1984

seven

That year the spring was blown into our town
On the fourth of February.
In antique uniform, looking rather a clown,
His horse speeding over the hard frozen ground,
He came—spring's emissary!
Then thunder rolled out to the ends of the land
As from muscles flexed in the sky;
And silvery horns of ghost regiment bands
Played the march soldiers hear as they die.
The horses advanced, chest deep in the spring,
The troops' cloaks got all muddy and wet,
While filling the air was a strange-sounding ring
That no one who heard could forget.
And my heart came alive at that ringing, it seems,
For my weariness melted away.
And this wasn't something I saw in my dreams,
For it was already day.

Есть праздник любования луной,
Так сказано в одной японской книге.
Подставить лоб под голубые блики.
Когда - не помню.
Кажется, весной.
А может, осенью, когда дозреет небо?
Как знать? В моем неласковом краю
Такое действо - невидаль и небыль.
Наверное, поэтому стою -
Привычно вопреки -
И жду минуты,
Когда взойдет
И медленной рукой
Погладит лоб,
И снизойдет покой
Со вкусом снега, вечера и руты.
Так мало между нами: лишь забор,
Сигнализация, два ряда заграждений
(Но не под током, кажется),
Да тени,
Которые свое происхожденье
Никак не прояснили до сих пор.
Еще решетка. Долго ли взойти,
Из проржавевших яростных колючек
Заботливо выпутывая лучик,
Неосторожно сбившийся с пути!
Оставь Земле ее докучный хлам,
Не обижайся на ее игрушки!
Давай-ка лучше из помятой кружки
Хлебнем воды за то, что ты взошла!
Теперь иди, срывая облака:
Все дерзостней, все звонче, все нежнее,-

eight

The Japanese reserve a holiday
To celebrate the moon, so reads my book,
To bask in moonlight, wonder, simply look.
Perhaps it comes in spring. They didn't say.
Or maybe fall, when earth brings forth her fruit.
While here in this—my harsh and unkind land—
Such things would be unthinkable pursuits.
No doubt that's why I've chosen here to stand,
Defiant still, impatient for the time
She'll come and stroke my cheek like some old friend
With gentle hand. And thus shall peace descend
And taste of rue and nights of snow and rime.
So little stands between us—just the wall,
Escape alarms, barbed wire in a double row
(Through which, I hear, the current's ceased to flow),
And shadows that in moonlight shrink and grow.
But cast by what? I cannot tell at all—
And window grate. Now moonrise is delayed
As mother Moon most carefully untangles
From barbed wire's sharp and rusted angles
Her errant child, a moonbeam that has strayed.
Leave Earth to play with toys not worth despising
Don't take offense at all this ugly clutter.
We'll raise a glass, though just a mug of water,
To celebrate our joy that you are rising.
Now go you forth and pierce the cloud:
Becoming ever bolder, clearer, purer—
With every breath more beautiful and surer,
Like girls in new high heels both shy and proud.
Now stop!
And bathe me in warm light.
I want so much to gaze at you till day.

Иди, с дыханьем каждым хорошея,
Как девочка на первых каблуках!
Теперь постой.
До дна зрачков согрей!
Я так хочу надолго наглядеться!
А что решетке никуда не деться -
Так сквозь решетку зрение острей.

1984

And though the bars will never fade away,
It's said that gratings sharpen up one's sight.

-Где я?

Идиотский вопрос.

Но, едва губами владея,

В кислород (ожог разряд купорос)

Возвращенные силой: -Где я?

Так и мне,

Не умея забыть черты,

За которой - ни псу, ни ворону,

Вновь проснуться: - Где?

И увидев: -Ты!

Согласиться - по эту сторону.

Ладно,

Будь - потолок чужой,

Будь неясно: Мордва ль, Италия,

Чей подъем - в озноб,

Чей рассвет - вожжой,

Чей тут гимн - ура, и так далее.

Пусть их.

Раз - на твоем плече,

Значит, дали еще свидание:

В этот серый свет,

В этот час ничей,

В это "здравствуй" - без оправдания.

1989

nine

Where am I?
What a question! Pathetic!
Yet when someone comes to (after failing to die)
Back from coma, shock, anesthetic,
He asks where (never how, never why).
And it's true of me too:
Still half lost in that realm, over there,
Where the beasts cannot go.
I wake up and ask: Where?
But just then I see: You!
And decide I am still here—below.
Very well! I agree to be here
Though this ceiling's not that of my home.
So what if it isn't quite clear
Whether this is Moldavia or Rome
In which I awake this chill dawn.
To the strains of some anthem's false pride
I will get in my yoke and go on.
Let it be! Since you lie at my side,
Since you're here in this room,
It must attest
That they're letting us meet once more.
In this morning's gray gloom,
In this hollow hour,
This "hello" that is worth all the rest.

Так закат воспален, что не тронь!
Ну так что же?
В общем, все хорошо. А детали -
Ну что же детали...
Мы давно не от мира газет,
Да словес, прилипающих к коже,
Да Иудиных цен.
Даже страхи - и те растеряли.
Мы давно отмолчали допросы,
Прошли по этапу,
Затвердили уроки потерь -
Чтоб ни слез и ни звука!
Мы упрямо живем -
Как зверек, отгрызающий лапу,
Чтоб уйти из капкана на трех,-
Мы освоили эту науку.
И с отважной улыбкой -
Так раны бинтуют потуже -
Мы на наши сомненья
Печальные ищем ответы.
А на наши печали - найдется трава...
Почему же
Так закат воспален,
Что глаза не сомкнуть до рассвета?

1984

ten

The red sunset, each night's, too inflamed to be touched.
What's the meaning of this to our lives?
In the main—all is well! And details? Of course,
That is harder to say. . . .
Quite some time we've not lived in the world of the news,
Of Judases, and the high price of betrayal,
Where words can pierce you like knives.
Strangely, even fear is gone.

It's been an age since they marched us away under guard
When we wouldn't give in or agree.
We have mastered the lesson of loss—
Don't cry, don't make a sound!
We live stubbornly like a beast in a trap
Who will chew off his leg to get free.
We'll do what we must to survive—
Our grades are quite high.

With a brave smile on our lips
We'll bind up our wounds more tightly.
We seek answers to doubts
Then discouraged, we poultice our sorrows.
But why then every night
Is the sunset inflamed
So we don't close our eyes till the morrow?

Ну вот и достали
Игрушки и свечи,
Оденем принцессу,
Осыплем дождем...
Поставим Шопена
И сказочный вечер
Одни, без гостей,
Не спеша проведем.
Достанем из ваты
Лиловую шишку -
И в хвойную гущу,
Чтоб руки в смоле...
И пахнет лимоном,
Медовой коврижкой
Да мятным морозом
Ребяческих лет.
-Ты помнишь?
-Я помню.
Как быстро стемнело!
И в сахарных листьях
Померкло окно...
Но длится наш праздник,
И что нам за дело
До старых печалей,
Уснувших давно!
Верхушку - звездою,
Подножье - простынкой,
А лапки - огнем,
Серебром, бирюзой.
Допела свеча
И остыла пластинка,
Но кружит мазурку

eleven

The ornaments, candles,
And tinsel are ready:
We'll dress up our tree
Like the Queen of the Night.
Let's put on some Chopin;
This fairy-tale evening
We'll spend without guests,
At our ease, tête à tête.
Let's take our glass pine cone
From its cotton swaddling
And hang it up first,
Let tar smear our hands.
The air smells of lemon
And honey cake baking,
The peppermint frosts
Of childhood's lost days.
"You remember?"
"Too clearly.
How quickly the night fell!
How windows were frosted
With spun sugar leaves."
Tonight we are festive.
Why should we look backward
At past griefs and sadness
We've long put to rest?
A star for the tree's hat
A sheet for its skirting
Green paws holding fires
The colors of jewels.
The candles go out;
The record has stopped.
But mazurkas still swirl

Стеклянный узор.
Сейчас ты закуришь
Движеньем привычным,
Я кофе налью
И к тебе подойду...
А елка грустит
И роняет реснички.
Но их подметут
В наступившем году.

1982

In frost patterns on glass.
And now you are smoking,
Your motions familiar,
While I pour your coffee
And move to your side.
The tree looks on sadly;
It's dropping its needles,
But we'll sweep them up
When next year begins.

Вот и кончена пляска по синим огням,
По каленым орешкам углей.
Вот и роздых оранжевым пылким коням,
А тепло все смуглей и смуглей.
Оскудевшей ладошкой остатки лови -
Не держи - отпускай на скаку!
Остыванье камина печальней любви,
Обреченней котенка в снегу.

А когда догорит, отлетит и умрет,
Как цыганский костер на песке -
То останется маленький грустный зверек,
Охвативший колени в тоске.

Что ж, не все танцевать этой долгой зимой,
Раз никак не кончается год!
И теряется в сумерках тоненький вой,
Унесенный в пустой дымоход.

Что ж, ни все баловаться, свиваясь кольцом,
Да хвостом разводить вензеля...
И хотелось бы года с хорошим концом,
Да остыла под лапкой зола.

Не скули, дурачок, мы газету зажжем -
Всю подшивку в разбойничий дым!
Хоть и мало тепла, да горит хорошо!
Потанцуем, а там поглядим.

1983

twelve

Now it comes to an end—this gay dance with blue flame,
Red-hot chestnuts turn back to charcoal.
Orange horses, once wild, have gone docile and tame
And the warmth, in the dark, has no soul.
Gather sparks with your hands, they're the fire's last breath,
But release them again. Let them gallop and go.
Even sadder than love is a bright blaze's death,
Worse than kittens left out in the snow.
When the flames have died down and the burning has ceased
Like last night's gypsy fire in the dawn,
Nothing's left of its soul but a small fire beast
Huddled up on the hearthstone—forlorn.
"This grim winter seems endless, I grant you, but still
You can't dance the whole cold season through."
Comes a cry in the twilight—pathetic and shrill
That drifts off and is lost in the flue.
"It's no use sulking there, all curled up in a ball,
Idly tracing your name in the soot. . . .
The old year may go out with a bang after all
Though the ash has gone cold under foot.
Do not whine, little fool, we've got newspapers here;
We can throw the whole stack in the grate.
Though it won't give much warmth, it will burn, never fear!
Now let's dance. All the rest leave to fate."

Пес, которого нет!

Пес мой,
Пес, которого нет!
Больше некому - залижи мне боль.
На нещаднейшей изо всех планет
Мне не страшно, пока с тобой.
Нам на шею камень - да в белый свет,
Где лишь ты - защита, лохматый мой.
Надо жить: не сказано, сколько лет.
Но потом обещано, что домой.
И туда нас впустят -
С тобой вдвоем,
Шкурой спасший меня от обид и бед.
Потому что там - настоящий дом,
Ты там - будешь,
Пес, которого нет!

1990

thirteen

Dog Who Does Not Exist

My dog,
Dog who does not exist!
I have no one else—come and lick my wounds.
On this, the most pitiless of planets,
I'm not afraid while I'm with you.
We're laden down and here in this wide world,
Where you are my only shield, shaggy friend,
We must live for who knows how much longer.
But then, so they promise, we can go home.
And they'll let us both in—
You can come too.
You, who have risked your skin
To save me from harm.
There you will live.
Dog who does not exist.

Когда мне исполнилось семь - не котенка в мешке,
Не стрелы и лук, не матроску,
                              не страшную книжку -
Мне дали в подарок наперсток по детской руке:
Блестящую штучку, оправу на палец-худышку.

И мне бы учиться шитью, постигая дела
Лукавых узоров, опущенных взоров и кружев...
Но я упирала иголку об угол стола:
Мой славный наперсток мне был не для этого нужен.

Я в нем подавала напиться усталым коням,
И мой генерал отличался блистательной каской,
И хитрая ведьма брала по ночам у меня
Все тот же наперсток -
                      летать в отдаленные сказки.

Тот год был печален, и новый, и новый пришел.
Пора бы умнеть. Но опять и опять полнолунье!
И я, непутевая, тычусь иголкой об стол.
А воины бьются, и лошади пьют, и летают колдуньи.

1982

fourteen

The year I turned seven I got for a birthday surprise
No bow I could shoot, scary book; oh no, nothing like that.
They gave me a thimble just made for a child of my size,
Which worn on my finger resembled a silvery hat.

Their hope was that I would be moved to love sewing, I guess,
And practice this feminine art form with coy downcast eyes.
Alas, my poor needle was left all alone on my desk;
I'd thought of a far better use for my fabulous prize.

I used it to water my steeds, who had galloped all day;
A helmet of silver became my best general's pride;
Each night a sly witch would come steal this same thimble away,
Then pilot it up to the stars after climbing inside.

That year was a sad one—the next and the next were the same.
High time I grew up! But each month the full moon lights the sky,
And then I abandon my needle and thread, without shame,
So armies can clash, horses drink, and my witch gets to fly.

Детство

На лестнице, пропахшей керосином,
На третьем марше, гулком, как орган,
Граненая стекляшка - как красиво!
Восторг сорок, поэтов и цыган!
Бывают ли находки вдохновенней?
Скорей надраить об рукав - и вот
На что ни глянь - сиреневые тени
И апельсинный радостный обвод!
Витки перил! Карниз! Лепные маски!
И нетерпенье прыгает уже:
Не пропадут ли сказочные краски
Вне мрамора и пыльных витражей?
Но милостивы сумрачные чары:
Двор - в леденцах!
О, с кем бы разделить
Открытие?
-Муркет! Смотри, котяра:
Какое солнце, аж стекло болит!

1982

fifteen

Childhood

Our stairwell reeked of kerosene and gas
But once between floors two and three, to my surprise,
I found a large teardrop made out of cut glass—
The kind that magpies, gypsies, and some poets prize.
What other find was ever so inspired?
I polished it a bit upon my sleeve and lo!
No matter where I looked were spots of lilac fire
Encircled by a joyous orange glow,
The curving banister, the fancy molding,
And yet, impatient child, I knew I must
Discover if these lights I was beholding
Could live without the marble stairway's dust.
Outside my fairy magic held its own.
The yard awash in candy-colored light.
How could I bear this wonder all alone?
"Here, Kitty, look! I'll show you such a sight!"

Ну, купите меня, купите!
Я такой хороший и рыжий!
Ну купите - и не любите,
Но возьмите к себе под крышу!
Я вам буду ловить мышей,
А если отважусь - крыс,
Домовых разгоню взашей
И приду на ваше "кис-кис".

Я буду вам песни петь,
Выгревая ваш ревматизм,
И на свечи ваши смотреть -
С подоконника, сверху вниз.
Заберите меня из клетки,

Я во все глаза вам кричу!
И не бойтесь нудной соседки:
Уж ее-то я приручу.

Откупите меня от смерти!
Ну кого вы еще откупите?
Вы вздыхаете, будто верите,
Сквозь решетку пальцем голубите,
Но уйдете, как все другие,
И не будет тепла и чуда.
О единственные!
Дорогие!
Заберите меня отсюда!

1989

sixteen

Won't you buy me, please, won't you buy me?
Don't you think that I'm sweet and pretty?
If not, even so, won't you try me?
I'll prove I'm a hardworking kitty.
I'll catch all the mice you could wish,
And even some rats if I'm brave.
I'll come when you call me "Kish-kish."
And make your house gremlins behave.

I'll purr my cat songs in your praise
And warm up your bones when it's chill.
At the flickering lights I will gaze
From my perch on the high windowsill.

Won't you please get me out of this cage?
Have eyes ever begged with more power?
Have no fear of your mean neighbor's rage—
I'll have her quite tame in an hour.

Please buy me and save me from dying.
Whom else could you rescue so cheaply?
I think you are moved, you are sighing;
I'm sure if you try me, you'll keep me!

But like the others, you're turning away.
My dreams of our life won't come true.
My savior, oh, what can I say
To get you to take me with you!

Сказки ходят на кошачьих лапах,
И от них смородиновый запах,
И они по ночам воруют:
Мальчиков,
              если плохо лежат,
Девочек,
              если плохо лежат,
Даже маленьких медвежат.
Озоруют, ох, озоруют!

А украденному - лес-малина,
Мост Калинов, а за ним долина,
И чего боишься, то будет.
Бабушка
            таращится: съесть,
Дерево
            цепляется: съесть,
В темноте волчьих глаз не счесть,
И никто-никто не разбудит!

Бойся всласть, а хочешь -полетели
Поскакать на облачной постели,
Звезды щекотать за усами:
Звон червонный,
                  жаркая медь!
Обожжешься -
                  чур, не реветь:
Там по небу ходит медведь,
Ждет потехи с гончими псами.

seventeen

Fairy tales creep on little cat paws
And smell like currants.
And by night they steal away
Little boys, if they don't go to bed properly,
Little girls, if they don't go to bed properly,
And even little bear cubs.
Oh, they are naughty, terribly naughty.

And they take the stolen child to the raspberry wood,
There is a honeysuckle bridge and beyond it a valley,
And whatever you fear, that's what they have there:
An old witch stares at you and eats you up,
A tree ensnares you and eats you up,
Wolves' eyes glow in the dark, too many to count.
And no one, no one will wake you!

Once you've had your fill of fear, you can fly,
Jump on a bed made of clouds,
Tickle the stars' whiskers:
A scarlet bell, hot bronze!
If you burn yourself, don't bawl:
There's a bear that patrols the sky
Waiting to have fun with the hunting dogs.

And from there you can see it all clearly:
The castles and roads and the chases.
Over there, the mermaids wave, laughing.
"Hey, you over there, behind the bronze mountain!
If you feel like a hero, come out and fight!
But if you're a coward we'll send you home,
You'll go back for ever and ever."

А оттуда - все, как на ладони:
Замки, и дороги, и погони.
Вот русалки машут, смеются.
Эй вы там,
            за медной горой!
Кто герой -
            выходи на бой!
Чур, кто струсит - тому домой
Навсегда-навсегда вернуться!

И потом реви под одеялом,
Вспоминай, как было - и не стало,
Только запах, как после грома.
Эй вы,
            звезды и голоса!
Вот я
            жмурю-жмурю глаза:
Украдите меня назад!
Все равно убегу из дома!

1999

And then you'll cry under the covers,
You'll remember how it was and is no more.
Only a scent, like after a thunderstorm.
Oh you, stars and voices!
Now I am closing my eyes tight-tight:
Steal me back there!
If you don't I'll run away anyway!

Как приготовить Землю

Так просто, так просто создать нашу Землю:
Пускай она странных сердец не приемлет -

Но в колоб тугой закатать, да покруче,
А то, что осталось, пустить бы на тучи

Немыслимых форм, сумасшедших изгибов -
Чтоб помнились мальчикам, грянув и сгинув.

Да зябких ракит подпустить наважденье,
Да льдам обозначить ночное движенье,

Да перечной россыпью птиц - на полсвода,
Да детского плача, да смутного года.

1988

eighteen

Recipe for a Planet

It's simple to whip up a world such as ours,
Although it's been said that it takes special powers.

Shape dough in a ball (only round loaves allowed),
The leftover scraps can be used to form clouds.

Make these rather fancy—with all kinds of swirls
For catching the interest of Earth's boys and girls.

Next bring on the willows, their magical lace;
Then chart a night course for the icebergs to trace.

Add sundry bright birds to enliven the air,
The cry of a child, and a year of despair.

Вот их строят внизу:

их со стенки можно увидеть.

(Ну а можно и пулю в невежливый глаз получить!)

Золоченые латы (это - в Веспасиановой свите),

Гимнастерки солдат, да центурионов плащи.

Завтра эти ребята, наверно, двинут на приступ.

И, наверно, город возьмут,

Изнасилуют баб -

И пойдет, как века назад и вперед, -

огонь да убийства:

Если спасся - счастливый раб, если нет - то судьба.

Храм, наверно, взорвут и священников перережут.

Впрочем, может, прикажут распять,

сперва допросив.

Офицеры возьмут серебро, солдаты одежду -

И потянутся пленные глину лаптями месить.

А потом запросят ставку: что делать дальше?

И связист изойдет над рацией, матерясь.

Будет послан вдоль кабеля

рвущийся к славе мальчик,

Потому что шальною стрелой перешибло связь.

А другая стрела его в живот угадает,

А потом сожгут напалмом скот и дома,

Перемерят детей колесом,

И стену с землей сравняют,

Но, возможно, не тронут старух,

сошедших с ума.

И не тычьте в учебник: истории смертники знают -

Прохудилось время над местом казни,

и хлещет течь.

Дай вам Бог не узнать, что видит жена соляная:

Автомат ППШ или римский короткий меч?

1984

nineteen

They're all formed up below:
>   climb the wall, you will see quite a sight.
(Though a bullet might strike your inquisitive eye as you gape.)
Gilded breastplates (these Romans get only the best when they fight),
The drab green of GIs, here and there—a red Crusader's cape.
In the morning these heroes are sure to attack at our gate
And no doubt our poor city will fall and the rapes will commence,
And the deaths, as in centuries past and in centuries hence.
If you live you're a slave, if you don't—
>   well that's fate!
Then they'll tear down the temple and savagely slaughter the priests
Or else crucify them once they've gone
>   through the famed "third degree."
Those in charge will take silver, the soldiers our clothes, at the least.
And they'll march prisoners off
>   through the mud on their bare bloody feet.
Next, to contact headquarters for orders on what else to do,
They'll try sending a cable, but arrows have shot through the line,
And despite all their cursing they "can't get a blasted thing through."
So they send some brash kid but he screws up and steps on a mine.
Then they'll get down to business
>   and napalm the buildings and stock,
Cull the kids with the wheel; raze the wall to the ground.
Perhaps sparing in mercy old women gone mad from the shock.
There's no history text where the tale of this siege can be found—
People sentenced to death know their history better than books.
Time wears thin and springs leaks
>   over sites of war's slaughter and blood.
For God's sake don't turn back—you'd be salt with one look
At AK-47s and muskets and short Roman swords.

У вулканов зловеще дымили кратеры.
Стерегли границы - и днем, и ночью.
Популярные римские императоры
Уменьшали плату своим доносчикам:
Вдвое, втрое - в меру гражданской совести.
Все дороги вели неизменно к Риму.
Вдоль дорог распинали. Из римских офисов
Шли приказы. Последствия были зримы
На крестах. Не надо валить на гуннов!
Пропыленным когортам светила слава.
Безнадежная цезарская фортуна
Улыбалась двусмысленно и лукаво,
Зная: каждый сей олимпийцам равен,
А по всем законам земли и неба -
Облеченный властью никак не вправе
Отказать доносчику в пайке хлеба.

1987

twenty

The volcanoes kept smoking—a sign of ill omen
They had guards at the borders all night and all day
Yet the emperors, courting the love of the Romans,
Failed to value informers, kept cutting their pay—
To placate the people—to a half or a quarter.
All the roads led to Rome then, or so Romans said,
But along these same roads, as the head office ordered,
Men were nailed up on crosses, left till they were dead.
(So why blame the poor Huns for decline and for fall)
Dusty cohorts brought glory to Rome when they marched.
Fortune smiled on the Caesars, but not kindly at all
And the look on her face was ambiguous, arch.
For though they'd attained near Olympian heights
They'd neglected a truth of both heaven and earth:
Though you've absolute power, you don't have the right
To deny your informers the wages they're worth.

Вот и стихли крики, Пенелопа,
Покрывало в сторону!
Он вернулся, твой высоколобый,
К сыну и престолу.
К лошадям своим и горожанам,
К ложу из оливы...
Ни разлучница не удержала,
Ни эти с Олимпа.
Вытер меч, сменяя гнев на милость,
Дышит львино...
Раз рука его не усумнилась -
Значит, нет невинных!
Всем злодеям вышло наказанье
От законной власти...
Вот рабыни смоют кровь с мозаик -
И начнется счастье.

1983

twenty-one

Come, Penelope, the roar's died out
Leave your loom, your weaving's done.
He has come back, ever tall, noble-browed
To his throne and to his son . . .

To his horses and his civic duty
His olive-wood bed made for love.
No force held him: not sorcery, not beauty,
Nor those from Olympus above.

As he cleaned his sword, his visage altered
Eyes and conscience clear.
Since his sword arm never faltered,
All deserved it who died here.

Wrong's avenged; true justice restored
Legal power holds sway.
Slaves wash the blood from the mosaic floor.
Happiness begins today.

Нарядили в тяжелое платье,
И прекрасною дамой назвали,
И писали с нее Божью матерь,
И клинки на турнирах ломали.
И венцы ей сплетали из лилий,
А потом объявили святой.
И отпели, и похоронили -
А она и не знала, за что.

1984

twenty-two

They bedecked her in satin and lace,
Gazing at her with worship and love,
Drew madonnas as having her face,
While at tourneys men died for her glove.
They wove lilies in wreaths for her crown,
Then they vowed that she was sanctified
And with hosannahs, put her in the ground.
Through it all, she had no idea why.

А вот и я, над газовой плитой,
В безукоризненном двадцатом веке -
Вся, до оборочки! Подделки никакой.
Четвертый час. Отяжелели веки,
Но теплится беседа, как свеча,
И не успеет догореть - как утро!
Мне возражают. Ласково и мудро.
А я упрямствую. Движением плеча,
И шепотом, и вот почти слезами -
Упрямствую!
Мне так немного лет,
Что я сужу, не пользуясь весами,
Но зная окончательный ответ.
И где уж мне за кофе уследить!
Вот он сбегает на плиту победно,
Безумствует, и пляшет, и чадит,
И дышит пеной из кастрюльки медной.
А я кидаюсь, обрывая спор,
Спасать!
И мы запутались руками...
Кофейный бунт подавлен.
Тихнет пламя,
И я опять несу упрямый вздор.
Мне возражают, ласково...
Нет силы!
Я вверх гляжу, дыханье задержав.
А впрочем, я давно уже забыла
И сущность спора,
И того, кто прав.

1982

twenty-three

Well, there I am; I'm standing at the stove
In nineteen something—the last century.
It's me all right in my outdated clothes.
My eyelids drooping; it's well past three.
Yet our dispute still burns on like a flame
That won't go out, nor will the daylight dawn.
I'm answered kindly, and yet all the same
Refuted; I am stubborn, argue on.
Impassioned, stifling tears of rage,
Certain what the final verdict has to be
Without the logic skills that come with age.
Thus occupied I've lost all track, you see,
Of how our coffee fares upon the fire.
And, sure enough, it now runs wild and hot
Across the stove in bubbling, steaming ire
Delighted to escape its jail-like pot.
Debate's cut off as to the stove I run.
Our fingers get entwined in the melee. . .
The coffee riot's quashed, debate is on
And stubbornly I leap into the fray. . .
Refuted kindly. . . forbidding tears to fall!
I hold my breath, and keep my eyes shut tight.
Now what we fought about I can't recall
Nor who he was—the man so wisely right.

Все дела заброшу -
Поминайте лихом!
Сяду на трамвайчик,
Поеду к портнихам.
        Чтоб захлопотали,
        Как куклу вертели,
        Чтобы сшили платье
        Цвета карамели!
Три моих портнихи:
Одна молодая,
Другая постарше,
А третья седая...
        Вот они над платьем
        Мудрят, как и прежде:
        Первая отмерит,
        Вторая отрежет,
        Третья на булавки
        Прикинет: любуйся!
        Иголкой прихватит
        И нитку откусит.
-Ишь, как засветилось!
Облако, не платье!
Надень без заботы,
Сомни на закате,
        Танцуй, с кем захочешь,
        Но попомни слово:
        Как разлюбишь сласти -
        Ты придешь к нам снова:
        За вечерним платьем,
        За цветом печали...
        Проводили садом
        И вслед помахали.

twenty-four

I'll abandon my work,
Let the world call it folly,
And go get a dress made.
Hitch a ride on the trolley.
      Let them twirl me around
      Like a doll, as they measure.
      Let them make me a dress
      In candy colors of pleasure.
I have three fine dressmakers:
The first young and gay,
The second one's older,
The third is all gray.
      They'll divide up the tasks
      Like before, I've no doubt.
      The first wields the tape.
      Number two will cut out.
      The third one, the gray one,
      Is an artist with pins.
      She takes up her needle
      And the magic begins!
"Oh, see how it shimmers;
It's a cloud not a dress!
Put it on, do not worry,
It won't ever get messed.
      Dance in it till morning.
      But heed what I say—
      You'll tire of sweets
      And come back here some day
      For a dress for the evening,
      The color of sighs. . . . "
      They walked me outside
      And they waved their good-byes.

Месяцы ли, годы
Буду вспоминать я,
Как меня кружило
Молодое платье,
Как одна смеялась,
Одна подмигнула...
Почему же третья -
Седая - вздохнула?

1984

This I'll remember,
For months, years—no less!
How I lost my head
To my merry, young dress.
How one of them laughed,
And the next winked an eye.
Only why did the third one,
The gray one, just sigh?

Как стеклянный шарик, невесть куда закатиться
(Уж кто-кто, а они всегда пропадают бесследно:
В самом трудном углу не найти,
Лишь пыль на ресницах,
Паучок на стене да кружок от монетки медной).

Закатиться, я говорю, где никто не достанет:
Там стеклянные шарики катятся по ступеням,
То ли сумерки, то ли ветер между мостами -
Словом, странное место, где я не отброшу тени.

Выше горла уже подошло: закатиться -
Ото всех углов, сумасшедших лестниц и комнат!
Не писать, не звонить!
Ну разве только присниться,
Как затерянная игрушка, которую днем не вспомнят.

1981

twenty-five

Oh, to roll, marblelike, to some lost corner God knows where
(For no matter what you do marbles vanish without trace:
You can search every nook—they're not there; only dust in the air,
A lost coin or two, and a cobweb that brushes your face.)

To roll off, I say, where I'll never be found by a soul
To a place where lost marbles have stopped their rolling at last
Where the light is dim or wind comes through each crack and hole
In a word, some strange spot, where my shadow will never be cast.

I'm fed up, up to here; it's time I rolled out of sight
Rolled away from each corner, crazy staircase, or chamber.
I won't call! I won't write!
Though I may show up in a dream some night
Like a child's lost toy that in daylight he doesn't remember.

Южный ветер

Долго ль, коротко здесь пробуду ли -
Нарисуй мне белого пуделя
Вот на этой,
Нещадно битой мячом стене,
Уцелевшей не то в ремонте, не то в войне.

И - да мир вашим стенам и кровлям,
Когда уйду,
И - да будет ваш город с водой и небом в ладу,
Чтобы ваша летопись -
Вся из целых листов,
Чтоб века струились меж кружевных мостов,

Чтоб ограды травой и мхом покрывал туман,
Чтоб цыганки отчаянно врали про ваш талан -
А сбывалось бы.
И чтоб синицы в садах,
Шпили - в тучах, и лебеди - на прудах,
Чтоб сквозь семь побелок наш пудель вилял хвостом.
Ну, а что тебе?
Расти. Я скажу потом.

1997

twenty-six

Southern Wind

How long I'll stay here, I cannot say
So draw a white poodle for me now, today
Right here on this wall that's survived war's assaults,
But now is bombarded by children with balls.

Peace to the walls and the roofs of your town
When I'm gone,
May you live on good terms with the land, sky, and sun.
May your chronicle hold
Only whole, unmarred pages.
May each filigreed bridge arch on through the ages.

May fog camouflage fences with moss, grass, and leaves;
May gypsies tell fortunes, too good to believe,
That come true.
May the spires reach to the clouds and beyond,
May there be larks in each garden and swans in each pond.
Through six coats of whitewash, may our poodle remain.
My wish for you?
When you're grown, I'll explain.

Северный ветер

Скоро будет прилив.
Сгонит отару вод
Северный ветер.
Сдвинутся корабли,
Небо вкось поплывет.
Что случится на свете?
Выгнется линзой свод,
Хрупкий взметнут балет
Птицы-чаинки.
Выступит мед из сот,
И покачнутся в земле
Чьи-то личинки.
Дети чужих зверей
Стиснут в мехах сердца -
Шорох по норам...
Ветер, то ли свирель -
Не угадать лица -
Будет, и скоро.
Знают сверчки небес
Рации всех судов,
Пеленг сосновый.
Нордом сменится Вест.
Смоется след водой.
Ступишь ли снова?

1984

twenty-seven

Wind from the North

Soon there'll be a sea change here.
From the north there'll come a tide,
Waters herded by the winds.
At a slant horizons veer,
Ships lose purchase, start to slide.
Sky's vault will be bent as by a lens.
What shall befall the earth, our home?
Birds, like tea leaves, whirl and roil
In wild and delicate ballet.
Honey runs out from its comb.
Restless underneath the soil
Churning larvae swarm and sway.
Trembling creatures in fur pelts,
Hearing something like a moan,
Feel fear pounding in their hearts.
Just the wind or something else?
Familiar faces seem unknown.
Any minute it will start.
Radar signals are sent forth,
For sky's crickets to decode,
From every vessel, every pine.
Winds will blow now from the north;
The tides all footprints will erode.
Will you walk here one more time?

Последний дракон

Плохо мне, плохо.
Старый я, старый.
Чешется лес, соскребает листья.
Заснешь ненароком-
                опять кошмары.
Проснешься - темень да шорох лисий.
Утро.
Грибы подымают шляпы.
Бог мой драконий, большой и добрый!
Я так устал:
           затекают лапы
И сердце бьется в худые ребра.
Да, я еще выдыхаю пламя,
Но это трудно.
         И кашель душит.
В какой пустыне метет крылами
Ангел,
      берущий драконьи души?
Мне кажется, просто меня забыли,
Когда считали: все ли на месте.
А я, как прежде, свистнуть не в силе,
Чтоб дохли звезды и падал месяц.
Возьми меня,
        сделай такое благо!
В холодном небе жадные птицы.
Последний рыцарь давно оплакан
И не приедет со мной сразиться.
Я знаю: должен -
          конный ли, пеший -
Придти, убить и не взять награды.

twenty-eight

The Last Dragon

I'm wretched and old;
Stiff joints and dull pain.
The forest sheds its dry skin like a snake.
If I drop off—
There'll be nightmares again.
Fox sounds pierce the dark, if I stay awake.
Morning. The mushrooms raise their caps to the skies,
God of the dragons, kind, good, and vast!
I am so tired.
Swollen paws, puffy eyes.
Beneath my thin ribs, my heart beats too fast.
Yes, I still belch flames with each breath,
But it's a strain.
I cough till I'm hoarse.
In what desert is he hiding that angel of Yours?
I trusted he'd come for my soul. What a joke!
I've been forgotten—just left off his list.
A broken-down dragon is easy to miss.
I wanted to call him, but no use to try;
My roar can no longer fetch stars from the sky.
God, in your mercy, please take me, I pray,
Why should the vultures keep circling in vain?
You know the last knight has long since passed away
And will not be coming to slay or be slain.
I know it is written he'll come with his sword
And kill me, with glory his only reward.
But why should I suffer? How can that be right
If Your creation was short by one knight?
All knights are at peace now: I ask You for no more.
It's hard to believe I've got into this plight.

Но я ль виноват, что рыцарей меньше
Ты сотворил,
                    чем нашего брата?
Все полегли,
А мне не хватило.
Стыдно сказать, до чего я дожил!
В последний рев
                    собираю силы:
За что я оставлен без боя, Боже?

1982

I'll summon my forces for one final roar:
God, why have I been left here with no one to fight?

Сегодня утро пепельноволосо.
И, обнимая тонкие колени,
Лениво наблюдает птичью россыпь
Во влажном небе. Бремя обновлений
Сегодня невесомо: ни печалей,
Ни берега в бездонной передышке!
Лишь ремешки отброшенных сандалий
Впечатаны в скрещенные лодыжки.
И безмятежный взор влекут осколки
Витых ракушек, сохнущие сети,
Песчинки да сосновые иголки,
Да звон и легкость бытия на свете.

1983

twenty-nine

Today the morning is ashy-haired.
And, embracing her slender knees,
Lazily watches the scattered birds
In the damp sky. The burden of renewal
Is weightless today; in this bottomless respite
There is no sorrow and no shore.
Only the straps of discarded sandals
Imprinted on crossed ankles.
And the carefree gaze is attracted to the fragments
Of spiral shells, drying nets,
Grains of sand, and pine needles,
And the resonance and lightness of being in the world.

Охота

Морозом пахнет от коня,
Заряжено ружье.
И не размокшая стерня,
А звонкий путь ведет меня:
- Скорей, скорей, - поет.
            Еще не езжена тропа,
            Как тихо дышит лес!
            Под ясным снегом сладко спать,
            Но нас выводит убивать
            Небесный знак - Стрелец.
Горя предутренним костром,
Его глаза светлы...
Мой хлоп играет топором,
И самородным серебром
Я зарядил стволы.
            Мой зверь залег, и нет следов,
            И стынут стремена.
            Но сердце чует дымный зов:
            Моя охота, как любовь,
            Смертельна и хмельна.
Глаза в глаза - мы встанем с ним
На свежий холст зимы,
И кровь прольется под одним:
Моя - лазурь, его - кармин...
Друг друга стоим мы!
            Я спешусь у твоих ворот
            И шкуру в дом внесу.
            А хочешь - пусть наоборот,
            И мой медведь меня убьет
            В серебряном лесу.

thirty

Bear Hunt

My rifle's loaded, close at hand;
The horses smell of frost.
The stubbled fields, the road, the land,
They lead me on, they sing, command,
"Come now or all is lost!"

The forest's breath is calm and still;
The sole footprints are ours.
How sweet to sleep in snow-soft chill,
But he has brought us out to kill—
The archer in the stars.

What do we need a fire for?
His eyes burn bright and hot . . .
My guide fingers his ax; what's more,
I've bullets made of silver ore
To use for my first shot.

He's gone to ground—no trace at all;
My beast is lying low.
Yet my heart hears his smoky call,
Intoxicated, held in thrall—
A hunt's like love, you know.

Into each other's eyes we'll stare,
But then the peace will shatter.
And one will bleed, I or the bear.
If we're well matched and it was fair
It really doesn't matter.

Легко дышать и сладко жить,
Но лес уже притих,
И пар над логовом дрожит.
Ты обещала ворожить -
Кому из нас двоих?

1982

Then home to you without delay
With fur to make a hood.
But things could go the other way;
The bear could slaughter me today
Within the silver wood.

The forest breaths a lullaby,
Steam rises from the lair.
Come get your cards and prophesy:
Which one of us is going to die—
The hunter or the bear?

Звери уходят от нас перед смертью -
И правы.
Травы стоят до последнего ветра -
И правы.
Мертвые чайки не ждут
Деревянной оправы:
Море колышет их перья
В разводах мазута.
Стертой монеткой мы купим
Забытое право:
Медленно выйти на берег
И ждать переправы -
С легкой душой,
Не печалясь о смене маршрута.

1987

thirty-one

Beasts go off alone before death.
So they should!
The reeds stand tall until the last storm.
So they should!
Dead gulls do not wait for
A coffin of wood
When the sea ruffles their feathers
In an oil slick of crude.
With worn coins we will buy
A forgotten good,
To go slowly out to that shore—
In a lighthearted mood
To wait for the ferry
Unworried by changes en route.

И снова в одиночество, как в воду,
С веселой жутью, с дрожью по хребту.
Кто остаются - мне простят уходы.
Уже так было.
Я опять приду.

Еще горят ожоги жадной суши,
Но губы леденеют глубиной,
И тишина до боли ломит уши.
И меркнет свет,
Ненужный и земной.

Пустые цифры дома-века-года
Смываются с былого бытия.
Там правит сердцем строгая свобода.
Там лишних нет.
Там только Бог и я.

И нет дыханья, чтобы молвить слово.
А только ждешь, что, может быть, опять -
Так редко с лаской, чаще так сурово -
Но прозвучит,
Что Он хотел сказать.

И все. И не позволит задержаться.
И даст посыл: как в поле со двора.
Ты знаешь, Господи, что я хочу остаться.
Я знаю, Господи,
Что не пора.

Но в судороге жесткой, как в конверте,
Выносит ослабевшая рука,

thirty-two

I plunge into aloneness yet once more
Elated, shivering, craven, I dive down.
They will forgive me—those I left on shore,
I've always come back
Safe, undrowned!

Though greedy fires of land still scorch and bake,
My lips are growing cool in sea-deep shade.
My unaccustomed ears in silence ache,
As useless lights of earth
Begin to fade.

The empty numbers: houses, dates, and charts
From past existence are washed off, erased.
And only freedom there controls my heart
Just God and I—
No more—within that place.

I have no breath, can't speak or make a noise.
But just await, in trembling joy and fear,
The mild (more often stern) sound of His voice
As He discloses
What I need to hear.

Now I must go: not linger on the way;
Take His dispatch to those I left at home.
You know, Oh Lord, how much I want to stay;
I know, Oh Lord,
My time has not yet come.

What is this message I am charged to bear?
Clenched far too tight within my shaking hand—

Что вложено в нее - для тех, на тверди:
Жемчужницу,
А может, горсть песка.

Не сразу и разжать.
Но, узнавая,
Но удивляясь, что еще стоят
Все в том же времени, и ждут у края -
Протянешь руку: что там, я не знаю.
Но те, кто ждали -
Те всегда простят.

1999

And brought unseen to those who're waiting there—
A pearl perhaps
Or a fistful of sand?

It's hard releasing my hand,
Letting go,
But, seeing them still standing there on shore,
I stretch my hand. What's in it—
I don't know.
But those who wait
Forgive me yet once more.

Песня полета

Так седлайте скорей, пока
Не начался рассвет!
Дорога недалека -
Всего лишь на тот свет.
Всего лишь один круг
От старых дорог Земли.
Мы будем там поутру.
За нами уже пришли.
И ноздри коней дрожат
Под счет последних минут.
Мы едем без багажа,
Сердца оставляя тут.
Так будем спешить, пока
Они не разорвались!
И шпоры - черным бокам,
Чтоб сразу - в гулкую высь!
Без пытки прощаньем - грянь
В глазницы, свод голубой!
Мы едем в такую рань,
Чтоб - ничего с собой!
Бессонный кромешный труд
И страх подойти к вратам -
Мы все оставляем тут,
Чтоб легче ответить там.
Чтоб, не отвернув лица,
В бестрепетный свет шагнуть -
Мы вам оставим сердца.
Сгодятся на что-нибудь.

1987

thirty-three

Flight Song

Saddle up, there's a glow in the east
By sunrise we must be gone.
Our journey's not long, at least—
We go just to the world beyond!
Which is only one orbit away
From old roads we've traveled before.
Those sent to show us the way
Are waiting for us at the door.
Horses sense that the moment is near
Nostrils quiver with haste to depart.
Our possessions will all stay down here;
We're leaving behind our hearts!
So let us start off on this ride
Before our hearts have time to shatter;
Dig our spurs in our mounts' black sides
And jump right off into ether
Avoiding the pain of good-bye
By leaving the earth at dawn.
We'll fly up into heaven's blue eye,
Not taking a thing along.
The hellish toil and the fear
Of appearing before these gates
Shall be left behind down here
To help us to deal with our fates.
So that into the light we may go,
Unflinching without excuse.
We'll leave you our hearts down below
In the hope they may be of some use.

И - в вечерний полет,
                  по-ребячьи раскинувши руки,
Словно в бездну, роняя затылок
                  в крахмальную стынь -
Пронесемся по снам,
                  ни в одном не уставшие круге,
В обомлевших ветрах наводя грозовые мосты!
Мы узнаем там тех, кого вспомнить пытались,
                            но меркла
У границы сознанья прозрачная память веков.
Мы в нее свою жизнь наводили,
                  как встречное зеркало,
Но глаза ослеплял свет неведомых нам берегов.
В озареньи полета мы будем бесстрашны и мудры,
И придут к нам крылатые звери
                  с небесных ворот...
А в кого превратимся, ударившись оземь наутро -
Нам еще неизвестно,
                  и стоит ли знать наперед?

1984

thirty-four

Now we'll plummet headlong
                    into night as into an abyss.
Arms spread childishly wide, from starched sheets
                        into dreams we shall fly—
Every orbit completed appearing to weary us less,
We'll lay bridges of lightning to stun every wind that blows by!
We will recognize those whose faces we knew in the past,
But whose images flicker just out of our memory's sight,
As from some other life we have led
                in the dream's looking glass,
Which our eyes cannot see
                since they're dazzled by day's blinding light.
In the dawning of flight we shall feel ourselves fearless and wise,
From the heavenly gates winged beasts
                will come eat from our hands.
But who we'll have become back on Earth
                    when next morning we rise—
No sense trying to guess,
              but then why should we know in advance?

Пропел петух,
Но ангел не трубил.
И мы живем на этом островке
Крутого времени.
Немного сохнут губы.
И дети бегают,
Которым всеми снами
Не утолить желания летать.
Какая сила
Их влечет к обрыву?

1991

thirty-five

The cock has sung
But angel horns are still.
We live on a narrow ledge above
The precipice of time.
We sense the end is near.
But, heedless, children run.
There are no dreams that will
Assuage their urge to fly.
What power then is this
Drawing them to the abyss?

Наши машины огромны и неуклюжи,
Как футболисты двадцатых - в трусах до колен.
Наши печали в обмотках бредут по лужам,
Наши тела называются словом тлен.
В наших садах одуванчики да крапива,
Как малолетние воры, вершат набег.
Нашим глазам - расплавить зло и счастливо
Тот, адресованный свыше, великий снег.

1990

thirty-six

Our machines are clumsy, outsized, prone to rust
Like an old-time ballplayer whose uniform sags.
While our bodies are rotting, returning to dust,
And our sorrows must trudge through the mud dressed in rags.
Weeds take over our gardens, invade and destroy,
Like young thieves staging raids on a neighbor's fruit grove.
But our eyes have the power, in rage or in joy,
To dissolve any snowstorm sent down from above.

Смейся, мальчик, у края Эреба:
Из погони, любви или боя -
Они все уходили на небо
И зверей забирали с собою.

О счастливые псы и медведи,
Как ваш табор кострами украшен!
Голоса и бряцание меди
Как мы слышим со спичечных башен!

Как нас там, в золотой круговерти,
Ждут, и дарят нам игры с огнями,
Раз молочные реки бессмертья
Шире ветра бушуют над нами!

Пусть под немощный бред асфоделий
Позабытые бродят обиды.
Из всех, что любили и пели -
Ни один не достался Аиду!

1990

thirty-seven

Rejoice, boy, at Hades' dark edge
From adventures, lovesickness, wars—
To the sky all the heroes have fled
Taking even their beasts to the stars.

Oh you fortunate bears, lucky hounds.
How resplendent your camp with its fires!
Merry voices and jangling sounds
We can hear from our frail matchstick spires.

On the gold carousel they are waiting
And catching a ring made of flames.
While eternity's river is raging,
They invite us to join in their games.

Let remembrance of injury, wrong
Be effaced by sweet asphodels' scent.
Those who've spent life in love and in song
For grim Hades realm never were meant.

Под созвездием Девы ручьи убегают в ночь -
И доносится смех, и возня весенних баталий.
Это было уже когда-то - давным-давно.
Кем мы были тогда, какие ветра глотали?
Эта черная легкость взмаха - каким крылом?
Этот шалый бег по остолбеневшим водам,
Этот странный озноб (апрель, и уже светло),
Эта получужая кровь - другого кого-то -
Затаилась, а вдруг взбурлит, понесет конем -
Не удержишь изодранных губ ни уздой, ни гневом!
И тогда, ничего не успев, лишь рукой взмахнем,
Но рука - уже не рука, и хохочет Дева.

1984

thirty-eight

Beneath Virgo's sign, streams plunge into dark, disappear;
Merry sounds of the spring's confrontations are borne to the ear.
Though it happened all right, it was long ago, lost in the past.
Who were we then in those days? What wild winds did we quaff?
That black weightless flash in the air, the sweep of what wing?
That mad, reckless dash over waves that had gone cold as stones,
That strange chill (it was April and light but nothing like spring),
That half-alien blood—not mine, but some person's unknown—
Lying dormant till then, it boiled up and began to rampage
And nothing could hold back that horse, not bridle, not rage!
For balance you throw out your arm; but one minute after,
Your arm's no longer your arm and you hear Virgo's laughter.

Блажен, кто не знает названья звезды,
Что ниже луны и хохочет, и пляшет,
Бесстыдно, как россыпь дешевых стекляшек,
Обманно, как шаг от судьбы до беды.

Блажен, кто не мучит начало пути
Под черные с белым дрожащие стрелки.
Бессмертные бездны играют в горелки,
И юным метелям концов не найти.

Блажен, кто смеется,
И имя свое
Горам прокричит, низвергая лавины,
И вспомнит земных виноградников вина,
Покуда плеча не коснулось копье.

А если коснется - не сметь обернуться,
На голос - очнуться, в полете - проснуться,
И глаз не поднять, и ни имени молвить -
Но встать, задохнувшись, и вечность исполнить,
Оглохнув от боли: падение в рост.

Блажен, кто не знает значения звезд.

1998

thirty-nine

He is blessed who won't learn what that star has been named
That cavorts and guffaws underneath the bright moon
Without shame, like a girl with cheap jewels festooned,
And deceives all of those who put faith in its claim.

He is blessed who won't follow a path that conforms
To the rule of his clock, the black hands on white.
Don't immortal abysses play tag in the night,
Deflecting the paths of the newly made storms?

He can laugh at the risk that he'll bring down a boulder
As he shouts out his name so the mountains resound.
He can relish the taste of Earth's wine he has downed
Till the moment the sword comes to tap on his shoulder.

And once he's been touched he won't dare turn his head,
He'll wake up in midflight to that Voice. Full of dread
He will not lift his eyes nor will he speak that Name,
But stand up out of breath, play eternity's game.
Numb with pain, the truth comes—that to live means to die.

He is blessed who cares not what the stars signify.

Опять дорога и опять закат.
Опять поля печальные лежат,
И родина чужая под ногами.
А кто-то там над нами молча ждет,
Напоминая о себе дождем.
Он знает все, что приключится с нами.
И сколько нам отмерено пути,
И то, куда нам велено дойти,
И что Он спросит, встретившись глазами.
А птицы чертят крыльями ветра.
А это значит, что и нам пора,
Но каждый путь мы выбираем сами -
Упрямее, чем прежде, во сто крат!
Опять дорога и опять закат.

1987

forty

Once more the road, as once again day dies.
Sad fields stretch out on either side,
With another nation's homeland under foot.
But Someone waits in silence up above
And sends us down the rain to show He's there.
He knows all our adventures, all our woes.
How many miles we've traveled on our way,
And where it's been ordained we shall arrive.
He knows what He will ask when our eyes meet.
Birds' wings are drawing patterns in the wind.
This seems to mean that our time too is near.
But we ourselves have chosen every road.
Each time we are more stubborn than the last!
Once more the road, as once again day dies.

Последние фонари

Меж рассветом и восходом,
Меж полетом и походом -
Вакварельный
Шершавый час -
Ветки робко копошатся,
Флюгера дохнуть боятся:
Кто там смотрит
На нас?

Кто там землю развернул -
Городом под кромку света?
Гаснут звезды и планеты,
Кто там смотрит -
На одну?

День был жаден - что ж, мы жили:
Прачки пели, швейки шили,
Лошадей гнали
Кучера.
Свечерело - вина пили,
Дамы вдумчиво грешили:
Вполприщура
Веера.

Кто заснул, кто не заснул -
Фонари потели светом,
Фитили шептались с ветром:
-Месяц, месяц...
-На блесну.

forty-one

The Last Streetlights

Between first light and start of day,
Between their flight and their mission,
In that watercolor, rough-hewn hour
Timid branches quake.
Weathercocks are scared to breathe—
Who's that watching us?

Who has turned the globe of Earth
To edge our city into light?
Extinguishing the stars and planets—
Who's that watching from above?

The day was greedy for our lives
And so we lived:
Laundresses sang,
Seamstresses sewed,
Coachmen whipped their horses.
When evening came
We drank some wine.
The ladies pensively sinned,
Fluttering their lashes and their fans.

Some went to sleep, some stayed awake.
The streetlamps oozed light.
The wicks whispered to the wind,
"The moon's a lure to catch a fish."
And then the night's fourth hour came,
The most terrible of all the hours,
The one that sees into our hearts.
And the babies cried

А потом наступил
Четвертый час -
Самый страшный,
Знающий все о нас.
И младенцы плакали,
Матери их кормили.
И тюремщики плакали:
Их ни за что корили.
И часы на башнях
Захлебнулись на третьем "бом":
Поделом умирающим
И рождающим - поделом.

Отошла ночная стража,
Отмолили спящих граждан
В отдаленном
Монастыре.
Спят убийцы и старушки,
Спят усталые игрушки,
Спят гравюры
Доре.

Вот и птичий час плеснул
Вхолостую по карнизам.
Чей-то голос:
-Эй вы, снизу!
Только город мой уснул.
Неповинный в рыжих крышах,
Драных кошках, гриппах, грыжах,
Грешный в том - не помню в чем,
В кружевах седьмого пота,
В башнях дедовской работы,

And their mothers fed them;
And the jailers cried
That they'd done nothing wrong.
And the clocks on the towers
Croaked on the third bong
To all those dying and giving birth,
"It serves you right!"

The night watchman retired;
The prayers for the sleeping were all said
In the monastery at the city's edge.
All the murderers
And all the old women slept.
All the little ones,
All the pretty ones slept.
Doré's engravings slept.

The hour came and the birds duly sang
And went unheeded.
Though one voice growled,
"Hey, you, down there!"
But the city had gone to sleep.
Not to blame for rusting roofs,
Or mangy cats, or influenza, or ruptures!
But still guilty of—
I don't know what.
It sleeps in lace acquired with the sweat of its brow,
It sleeps in the towers its grandfathers built,
Well versed in the fact
That everything has its price.
Feeling itself safe behind double-glazed windows,
Having glut its maw, and drunk its fill,

Искушенный,
Что почем.

Застекленный от тревог,
Пиво пивший, брашна евший,
Трижды начисто сгоревший -
Он себя не превозмог.

Вот и спит,
А уже пора.
Транспоранты и прапора -
В тряпки выхлестаны,
И фитили
Просят гибели: утоли!
Кто там смотрит:
Стоит ли утру быть?
Литься ль облаку,
Чтобы птицам пить?
Пусто глазу в кровлях -
Сто снов окрест,
И никто не крестится
На уцелевший крест.

Только мокрой мостовою,
Только кровлей листовою -
Ангел ветра
Да ангел зари.
Да в засаленной одежке
Наш фонарщик тушит плошки
И последние
Фонари.

1998

Having burned to the ground thrice
But now unable to rouse itself once again.

So it sleeps on,
And it is already time.
The advertisements and the banners
Have been whipped to tatters
And the wicks beg for oblivion,
"Put us out!"
Who's that watching, wondering
If it's worth another morning?
If the rains should fall
So birds can drink?
For a hundred dreams around
The roofs are empty
And no one cares to pray
To the one cross that survives.

Only over damp pavements,
Only over the leaves on the roofs
Walks the angel of the wind,
Walks the angel of the dawn.
And our lamplighter,
His clothes greasy from lamp oil,
Puts the last streetlights out.

Где я видела мокрую ветку на стертых камнях,
И торговку черешнями в шляпке немыслимых роз,
И кофейню с железным ангелом на дверях -
Где я видела?
Безнадежный вопрос.
Я не помню даты, врезанной во фронтон,
Я не слышу города, что грустит по моим шагам.
Мне пора идти,
Оставляя все на потом:
На бессонницу через сотню лет -
Плач по тем берегам,
Что когда-то стыли вечером, сохла соль,
А волна целовала руку и умерла.
Все дорожки к месяцу отливали в смоль,
А одна уводила вверх и была бела.
А вослед звенели окнами допоздна,
Но уже голоса кузнечиков и детей
Становились меньше,
И капала тишина.
Только плакал старый трамвайчик между путей.

1982

forty-two

Where was I when I saw a wet branch against stones worn smooth
Or a woman with impossible roses on her hat selling cherries
Or a wrought-iron angel above the door of a café?
Where was I when I saw. . . . Impossible questions
I cannot recall dates carved into marble and stone
I can no longer hear the sounds of the city that longs for my step.
It is time to go, all else I must postpone
For some sleepless night in the far future—
Weeping for those shores that grew chilly at sunset
The salt dried and the waves kissed my hand and died.
All roads to the moon were coated with black tar
All except one white path.
I heard neighbors' windows bang late into the night.
Slowly the voices of children and crickets grew still.
Silence fell by drops
Until far off a trolley car whined.

Когда-нибудь, когда-нибудь
Мы молча завершим свой путь
И сбросим в донник рюкзаки и годы.
И, невесомо распрямясь,
Порвем мучительную связь
Между собой и дальним поворотом.
И мы увидим, что пришли
К такому берегу Земли,
Что нет безмолвней, выжженней и чище.
За степью сливы расцветут,
Но наше сердце дрогнет тут:
Как это грустно - находить, что ищем!
Нам будет странно без долгов,
Доброжелателей, врагов,
Чумных пиров, осатанелых скачек.
Мы расседлаем день - пастись,
Мы удержать песок в горсти
Не попытаемся - теперь ведь все иначе.
Пускай победам нашим счет
Другая летопись ведет,
А мы свободны - будто после школы.
Жара спадает, стынет шлях,
Но на оставленных полях
Еще звенят медлительные пчелы.
Ручей нам на руки польет,
И можно будет смыть налет
Дорожной пыли - ласковой и горькой.
И в предвечерней синеве
Конь переступит по траве
К моей руке - с последней хлебной коркой.

1983

forty-three

The time will come, the time will come
We'll silently complete our trek.
Throw down our packs and years upon the beach grass.
Then, weightless, straighten up again.
We shall cut the painful cord
That ties us to the road's next turn
And we shall see we have arrived
On earth's far shore. Nowhere is there
A place more parched, more silent, or more pure.
Beyond the steppe the plum trees bloom,
And yet our hearts tremble here.
How melancholy it is to find what we've been seeking.
How odd to live with nothing owed,
Without our friends, without our foes.
No feasts in time of plague, no frantic races—
Our days unhitched, let out to graze.
We will not try to hold sand
In our fists. All is now altered.
Let someone else keep up accounts
Of victories that we have won.
But we'll be free like children out of school.
The heat abates, the path grows chill
But on the abandoned fields
The slow bees are still buzzing.
And streams will pour over our hands
Thus washing from them every trace
Of our long journey's merciful but bitter dust.
And in the evening's bluish light
A horse will walk over the grass
To beg our last dry crust of bread.

Открываю старую книгу
И читаю никому не нужные вещи.
Никому, кроме, может быть, ненормальных,
У кого болит то, чего нет,
Справедливо называемых психами.
Это в нашем веке было такое ругательство.
В очередях.
Открываю, а они уже теснятся:
Все невидимые глазу тени,
Что ведут бессонницу в поводу. А бессонница
Хочет пить.
Эти знают, эти напоят.
Завлекут, затанцуют, заморочат.
Чур вас, чур, конокрады!
У меня артерии - сонные. Не по адресу, господа.
Вот чайник: электрический, сам выключается.
Вот столик: кофейный, и для журналов.
Радиатор исходит теплом.
Закройте книгу, сквозняк
С этого разворота, где волосок завитком -
Неизвестно чьим.
Может, просто читала и обронила -
Какая-то она,
Семдесят лет назад.
Или боялась обыска, проверяла.
Знаменитая проверка на волосок:
Если выпал, заложенный -
Значит, книги трясли.
Кто же она была,
С завитком, еще не седым?
Я знаю, была одна:
За ее спиной переглядывались,

forty-four

I have opened an old book
To read things no one cares about any longer.
No one except, perhaps, abnormal people,
Those who suffer pain in organs that do not exist
And thus are rightfully referred to as psychotics.
This word has become a curse in our era,
Especially among people standing in lines.
So I open this book, and they all come crowding in:
All these shadows the eye cannot see,
Leading insomnia in on a leash. But insomnia
Wants a drink.
As they knew he would; they get him drunk.
Lead him on, make him dance, play him for a fool.
"Be off, be off, you horse thieves!"
No one steals my sleep.
You've come to the wrong place, my friends.
Look, here's my teapot: it's electric and turns itself off.
Here is my table: for coffee and magazines.
The radiator is putting out heat.
Close the book, there's a draft
Coming from the open page
On which there lies a wavy hair—
How would I know whose hair?
Maybe, some woman was reading
And it simply fell on the page
Seventy years ago.
Or perhaps she feared a search and placed it there.
This was a well-known tactic:
If it was gone, the hair between the pages,
It would mean the book had been tampered with.
Who was she, wavy haired, not yet gray?
I know of one woman

Но царственно, смехотворно, неукоснительно -
Она проверяла на волосок
Все свое состояние в странных буквах нашего века:
Ежедневно,
Как чистить зубы.
А потом шла стоять в свою очередь.
Впрочем, волосы ее не вились.
Стало быть, это другая
Обронила
Случайно.

1999

Who was under surveillance
But who, regally, ludicrously, unfailingly,
Placed a hair in each of her books—
Her whole estate—written in the strange letters of our age,
Daily,
The way she brushed her teeth.
And then she went out to stand in line.
But that one's hair wasn't wavy.
So it must have been someone else
Whose hair fell here by chance.

Тот ветер, как и смерть, приходит сверху.
Он городам ломает башни и гробницы.
Он смахивает крошки самолетов
С разодранных небесных скатертей.
И вожаки кричат последнюю поверку,
И отвечают им измученные птицы,
Теряя одержимость перелета,
Уже с паденьем
В сломанном хребте.

Зачем нам знать, что этот ветер будет?
Ведь мы не лезем с микрофонами к пророкам,
Зато достигли мудрых философий
И пластиковых банковских счетов.
И вожаки людей успешно вышли в люди,
И суррогаты апельсинового сока,
И чашки обезвреженного кофе
Нас ждут в любом
Из аэропортов.

Неважно, где. А важно, что под крышей.
Еще желателен хороший курс валюты.
В любое место выдаются визы,
В любом отеле мягкая кровать.
И если птицы закричат, мы не услышим.
Лишь иногда бывает зябко почему-то.
И мы тогда включаем телевизор
И смотрим жутик,
Чтоб спокойней спать.

1999

forty-five

That wind, like death, will swoop down from above
And smash up cities, all their tombs and all their towers.
That wind will scatter aircraft, like cake crumbs,
From off the tattered sky-blue tablecloth.
Bird leaders summon flocks for one last roll call.
The tortured birds will answer one last time but barely,
No more obsessed with the need to migrate,
And so they fall
Go crashing down to earth.

Why must we know just when that wind will come?
It's not as though we make our prophets heroes.
Although we've all acquired wise philosophies
As well, of course, as plastic credit cards.
By now our leaders have all found themselves places.
And cups of acid free, decaffeinated coffee
And artificial orange juice in boxes
Await us all
At any airport.

It's not important where, if there's a roof above.
A good exchange rate doesn't hurt either.
For any place on Earth they issue visas,
And every place the hotel beds are soft.
And if the birds cry out in pain we do not hear them.
Though sometimes, for no cause, we're seized with terror.
But there's a cure for that. Turn on the TV
And watch a horror show
To help you sleep.

О ветер дороги, вслый и волчий!
Сквозняк по хребту от знакомого зова.
Но жаркою властью сокрытого слова
Крещу уходящго снова и снова:
-С тобой ничго не случится плохого.
Вдогонку. Вослед. Обязатльно молча.

Меня провожали, и я провожаю:
-Счастливой дороги.
-Ну сядем. Пора.
А маятник косит свои урожаи.
Мы наспех молчим, а потом уж рубаха
Становится мертвой и твердой от страха -
Не сразу. Не ночью. В четыре утра.

Но страхи оставшихся - морок и ложь.
Терпи, не скажи, проскрипи до рассвета.
Не смей нарушать молчаливое вето,
И ангелов лишней мольбой не тревожь.

А если под горло - беззвучно шепчи
Про крылья, и щит, и про ужас в ночи.
Он стольких сберег, этот старый псалом:
Про ужас в ночи
И про стерлы, что днем.

1998

forty-six

Oh, wind of long journeys—wild, gleeful, and proud.
How often I've felt your cold breath on my spine.
As loved ones to gods of the road I consign,
Pronouncing in silence like some magic spell,
"Let nothing bad happen. May all turn out well."
Such words may protect them, though not said aloud.

Someone's always leaving for places unknown.
"Godspeed. Bon voyage. Get on board—there's the warning!"
So does the pendulum reap what's been sown.
Last minute farewells disappear in the hurry.
It's not until later we're flooded with worry,
Awakening trembling at four in the morning.

But terrors like this felt by those left behind
Are merely deceits to be borne, I have found.
Endure them in silence, do not make a sound.
Don't bother the angels with pleas of this kind.

And if you can't stand it, then silently sing
The psalm about refuge beneath the Lord's wing.
Those words keep all manner of dangers away:
Like terrors by night and arrows by day.

Notes to the Poems

Three, page 7

The growing of the soul is taken from Orthodox terminology. It means not making sacrifices, but living for God's glory. That is not only serving God, but becoming immortal in the process. At the same time this is both painful and joyful. Connected with this thought are the images of spring—clouds looking at us and the smallness of our temporary home, planet Earth.

From the window of the railcars as we travel south in the spring we can see the children outside in their swings playing in the sun.

Four, page 9

Orange peels are typical winter/spring rubbish in the narrow port streets of Odessa.

Five, page 11

This poem is about the spring mood. In Russia, the time when ice breaks and rivers are free to be navigated again is the time to change from sledges to boats. Thus, it is good to see the oar once more.

Six, page 13

I'm not sure this poem will make sense to Americans. It is about the Soviet spring and the contrast between spring freedom and isolation. No news—there were times when letters were confiscated, the radio was jammed, and telephone conversations were controlled. People felt completely cut off from the rest of the world, including their friends.

Seven, page 15

The general meaning of the poem is that one nasty winter morning while I was in the Soviet camp I looked out the window and crossing the fields I saw phantom troops in Russian uniforms of 1812 (the Napoleonic Wars). The soldiers were wet and dirty with snow melted beneath the horses. I heard trumpet sounds full of promise. In myself I felt that victory was close, winter was almost over. I still cannot make out whether it was a vision or a hallucination because I was starving in my cell and only half alive. In Russia this poem was made into a song.

Nine, page 21

I had a near-death experience in my punishment cell, and as is often the case, I came back with a better appreciation for this place. In my dreams I go there again, and upon waking up, the first moment I must ask myself, "Where am I?" It takes great effort to sort out exactly where I am—which world, which country, which hotel or prison. I am glad to accept this world because I am together with the man I love.

Eleven, page 25

Why decorate the tree after Christmas? You see, our Orthodox Christmas is on 7 January. That's why many people decorate the tree on New Year's Eve, before Christmas comes.

In Russia we keep the glass figurines in big boxes, each wrapped in cotton wool, and it is a great joy, especially for the youngsters, to unwrap them, half-forgotten through the year. All these years those things were stored in Kiev waiting for us to return.

Nineteen, page 45

As I mentioned, the destruction of war, that cycle of history, has been repeated many times over the centuries. The outcome is always the same.

During Mongol times when a city or town was taken by Orda, the Russian children were measured by the wheel of the Mongol's cart. Those who were taller than the wheel were killed, the rest were taken as slaves.

Twenty, page 47

The meaning of informers in this poem is as negative as it can be. The word means either KGB-type agents or amateurs who informed on the people to the government, expecting a reward. The whole thing is meant to be sarcastic. —Lydia Razran Stone

A state built on lies, spying, and cheap tricks will weaken and destroy itself. No amount of bureaucracy, military forces, or boasting propaganda can save it from failing. —Irina

Twenty-one, page 49

I have always been suspicious of happy endings. The idea of this poem is what happens after rightful revenges—they simply do not stop. The temporary relief after revenge is a poor reason for happiness.

Twenty-six, page 61

The picture I had in mind with this poem was a conversation between the wind and a young artist, a child with a crayon, perhaps. We all used to understand the wind tongue when we were young.

Thirty-six, page 87

I think it is hard to understand the whole meaning of this poem without European experience of two world wars. When Odessa was occupied by Romanians under German support in the Second World War, the citizens did not take the soldiers seriously because their officers wore low boots with pieces of cloth wrapped around them, a sign of poor army supplies. Our officers wore high boots to the knee with their trousers pushed inside. For years after the war people used to wear what was left of the military uniforms; these leg wrappers meant the lowest level of poverty.

The power of the eye. What is meant is that we all know a good teacher can quiet a class with one glance, animals often perform under its trainer's gaze, some people claim they can supernaturally move things just by looking, and there are many stories about the saints who stopped the murderers, saw what happened far away, stopped fires and what not. Whether it was done through eyes or with mental power is not important. But what we can see is people's eyes, and often they tell us a lot about their owners' strength.

Forty-four, page 107

The woman mentioned in this poem is most likely Anna Akhmatova, a very well-regarded poet in Russia during the Silver Age (approximately 1894–1922). She is considered one of the finest Russian lyric poets, and perhaps the finest female Russian poet of all time. Anna Akhmatova's poetry kept the memory of pre-revolutionary Russian culture alive when the government was trying to destroy it. Akhmatova also kept alive the memory of the victims of "the terror", the name given to the political purges under Stalin. —Jane Hertenstein